A Mule C

By Liza Charlesworth

ISBN: 978-1-339-02780-7

Art Director: Tannaz Fassihi; Designer: Tanya Chernyak
Photos © Getty Images and Shutterstock.com.
Copyright © Liza Charlesworth. All rights reserved. Published by Scholastic Inc.

1 2 3 4 5 6 7 8 9 10   68   32 31 30 29 28 27 26 25 24 23

Printed in Jiaxing, China. First printing, August 2023.

■SCHOLASTIC

This mule is so cute
and it is a big help.
A mule is a nice pet!

mane

nose

A mule has a mane.
A mule has a fine nose.
It can smell well!

Mules drink fresh water.
They graze on grass.
Munch, crunch!

Mules like to do jobs.
We can use them to help us
lug huge packs.

We can use mules to help us
get to the top of a path.
Clip, clop, clip, clop!

A mule can step on rocks.
It can trot on grass.
It can jump and kick.

Mules are so cute
and they help us a lot.
A mule is the best pet!